D1189532

The Sunrise Liturgy

The Sunrise Liturgy

A Poem Sequence

MIA ANDERSON

For my family
with love from
Mia
March 2013

WIPF & STOCK · Eugene, Oregon

THE SUNRISE LITURGY
A Poem Sequence

Wipf & Stock
An Imprint of Wipf and Stock Publishers
199 W. 8th Ave., Suite 3
Eugene, OR 97401
www.wipfandstock.com

ISBN 13: 978-1-62032-016-7
Manufactured in the U.S.A.
Cover Photo © Mia Anderson.

for Tom, twin, always

and for Rowan

Contents

Caveat lector

Over and over.
You have entered this life?
Be warned.

Over and over the sun.
You grew up perhaps
with the cow [jumped]

over the moon.
This is different. Here you will find
the sunrise liturgy.

Here you will find things repeating themselves.
Even first times repeat themselves
as first times.

You think all this
iterating iteration is a version of
hell? It is heaven

for those for whom it is heaven.
Things don't come clearer.
We are two species

the hell species and the heaven species.
I don't say we can't inhabit both.
We have dual citizenship.

I just wanted to warn you.
This is the sunrise liturgy and mostly it is heaven.
This is for those for whom it is heaven.

Dayspring : you before
       at spring of day, at first
jump of sun using the horizon as a spring-board.
Or the spring-board itself.
Or an invite to a Jump-Up.
Or day's season of beginnings — daily freshening source
       of wave or particle.

'The night has passed and the day lies open before us....'
Start of every morning. Day like a book flat on its spine
       pages to left of you pages to right
wide
       open
readable but not read.

A slice of horizon with a lid of sky on a plate of water
            le fleuve, ever-moving, flowing towards
       the read pages, away
    from the unread
ever-passing, time's model.

Your eye, reading. Horizon a blink
the far shore the eye-lid with its lashes, the near shore the lower lashes
       you the pupil in the middle
at your *paedeia*, scanning, duty at its delight the Other Book before, learner
with your beginner's licence, blink, and the colour has changed
      like a carousel of old-fashioned slides, blink, and the flame
         has gone rose, the rose peach, the peach
           gold, the gold ivory and luminous cream, and *then* —

Brother Sun has sprung

pop-up jack-in-the-biodegradable-box of night
coming up from down-under
gasping for air as he clears the watery *fleuve*.

The people that walked in darkness, or stumbled from bed to bath or
       wandered sleepless groping for texts like capsules
have seen a great light, Brother Sun leaping like a Lord
the sun of righteousness arising
                      my! — but
that Charles Wesley could sing!

'Christ, whose glory fills the skies' can you hear the tune?
                 'Dayspring
          from on high, be near;/ Day-star,
     in my heart appear.'
Almost 200 years of it flowing by
            no one dipping in the same tune twice
     the same always anew.
Like the light.

Liturgy : the solemn procession
of numinous vapour off the *fleuve* festooning the minus 35 degrees
             as it glides downstream
         an armada dedicated to self-annihilation
     in the *Sol Glorianus* :
Christ whose glory fills the skies, Light from Light.

Dayspring : the time of first take on 'the fair glory'
       linking the light within with the light without.
The people who walked without light
have seen a great light.
And eaten it
with their eyes.

Day within.

How dawn

Look. Look. You see?
— how dawn
like a benign flesh-eating disease
invades the shrinking dark,
devours.
The dark shrinks, cowers
behind small objects,
huddles, hurls itself
away from tall trees, the lawn's
a line-up of escapees.

It does no good.
Like Mr Todd.
The sun will trump you every time, Mr
Wind-Who-Would blow Todd's coat off.
It doesn't work that way.
Sun beams, it beams.
Dawn. Coats off.
And the dark is gone.

There. See?
Think when it began, when you
could not be sure whether
light had begun or your dream continued.
The benign infection advanced cell by cell
into the body of night, till you could not tell
if you could see
or you could not see.
But you could.

The infarction of love.
Poor dark night. It happens every time.

MIXED MESSAGE

Half past dawn for us mixed mortals
　　　and the frozen birch tree is doing as good a job
of feeding the grosbeaks as the frozen apple tree.

When they swirl away from their *délices de sorbet aux pommes*
　　　(McSorbet) in the winter sun
they head for the top of the birch and snack on its catkins.

　　　Of the five, two
have red breasts, sharply V-shaped sharp red and
they are pecking themselves, those two,
strenuously pecking their breasts…

can this really be grooming?
Isn't that blood they're feeding on? 'Struth!
　　　I know it's cold out, but.

Ah, they fly away, with the others,
　　　as living as ever.
Flip the pages. The rose-breasted grosbeak… sure enough
a V like a dagger in the chest.

Have you heard the one about the pelican?
Mother pelican performs own breast surgery, beak like a dagger,
feeds its young
　　　with gobs of its own blood.

Have you heard the one about the pelican chick?
An insurance chick gets laid, one egg alongside the favoured egg
　　　and when the favoured egg hatches and thrives
the 'insurance chick' gets pushed out of the nest.
That's it for the chick.
　　　For this it came.

So which is for real?
Both are. Different iconographies.
In the Other Book it's the iconography of fittedness —
        multiple wasted experiments of how to get along in this world.
        A zero sum game,
it worked for pelicans.

        Pelican so loved the world
        that she gave her other begotten one, to the end.
        Now all that believe in Pelican
        shall not see 'Pelican' perish but have persistent life.

In the book that's called The Book, it's science lesson 101
        before the burning bush : 'Turn aside.'
See why the branches are not consumed.
'Wisdom :
        attend!'

Asidedness.
The grosbeak as burning bush
        step one on the marathon of self-offering
                that burns and burns and is not consumed.

The iconography of cathedral glass, bronze, stone,
        Latin's *Pie Pelicane,* the ancient christic image.
And we : in the image, we say. Pelicans unlimited.

'We offer and present unto thee… ourselves, our souls and bodies,
        to be a reasonable, holy, and living sacrifice…'
(Cranmer's 16th century take on Paul of the Book).
        You mean *really*? You mean *do*?

As a race, we have a pretty clear notion of where
        one skin stops and another begins. We're good at boundaries.
We could push the chick from the nest — we're
        the favoured chick.
My pain is not yours, and vice versa.
At least we live as if that's what we thought.

But the pelican of Christology and legend, that's
     a horse of another feather.
Someone called it
     'absolute donation.'
What if

drawing your own blood to feed others
     blood donorship in clinical quiverfuls of mystic syringes
          what if *sheer* cliff-edge generosity
     absolute donation
were the bull's-eye of every post-communion prayer? For real?

I think we might lose our sense of skin, of whose pain is whose,
     of where
          the edge of the nest is.
That would be novel.
We might feel the pain of the Congo.

Or would that be asking
     more than we're up for?

RIVERBREATH

Before there's light, there's a wall of black halfway up the sky
glooming as if a distant storm-cloud
     had rolled in
   or been rolled out
  then lodged
on top of the far shore.

Or had it made it that far? Or both far and away beyond?
    Who was to know.
  There was no light to see by
just black on black.
Would something crash soon, something break or burst —
    down or forth or out?
  Who knew.
Sleep rolled around.

Closer to dawn, a windowful of blank, etched on by naked trees :
dance still as still life, *nature morte*. The blank : full
so full the foghorns must sound,
the coast guard and freighter invisible in the breath of the river.

   The riverbreath had begun to precipitate out at first on the
    topmost branches
     the fingers in this still dance
   fitting the tips before lightfall with gloves as light as breath
    divinable if doubtable;
    but now
   while the sun's own foghorn oooood its retinal signal of potential
    to our intimations of sunrise and
    the Imminence
   began to burnish the backside of the grey,
    the mist
    emboldened
   feathered the fingers further with fur, rime no longer doubtable
    no less than
    visible and risible now

on the poised dancers, whose dance is… in this
retina skittering over their limbs.

The sleep of night rolls over,
likes the feel,
rolls again
rolls the riverbreath round like cud in its mouth
intestinefuls of cud that stretch out the length of the riverrun seaward
rolling, rolling
curling like unwound cud downstream
chew-chew! le *train-train* of rivering dawn mist
fed by imminent sun
you think I'm joking? fanciful? I say it like I see it.

Now immanent sun's sunning up the -rise
risible and visible
and the riverbreath coating the mirror, haa-haaaing on the
mirror of us, shoreline, and us, *riverains*
all the breath's neighbours and all the breath's men
on whom the precipitate of river falls like… a baptism

a condensation of dawn. The Sun Effect :
blessed, graced, manna'd, this white fallout, this alter-precipitate
of light with voice like a foghorn,
herald of the down train.

Tin coin of sun
having mustered the wattage to burn through the grey
is gold sovereign now at break of day
and about its business of doubling and redoubling the helix of
mist twisting downstream
towards town and gown, master of ceremonies of this
mystic parade
of evaporating banners
lord of the ephemeral
His Eminence
Lord of the Things.
Mistagogy.

SHORELIGHT

It's shorelight you're seeing,
the sky performs a metaphor
for you
(like Chaplin putting his bowler hat
under the bed at bedtime)

the riverrun of sky this time (every time) being
our life lived, with banks or *berges*
in need of shearing. Did you know
shore comes from shearing?
Imagine.

Dawn's twilight sees us
shorn of our matted dreams
disembarrassed of our shag by our *bergers*
and shivering with expectation
at the fringe of the day
like sheep

or else sheep waiting to be driven
into the flood to wash their wool wool-white
after the treatment —
liminal
Hebridean for now, and blinking at it all.

So that great band of orange in the sky
is a sandbank and seems to bank
the choppily skidding sky
but it's your life it's banking on.
Really.

And all our life we're just part
of a shore people who were born to this,
for this.
We grew up here aquatic apes,
youngster apelets each of us once

hanging onto our mother's every hair
and she weaving the shallows, the littoral
a few million years ago.
Seems like yesterday.
Hope

so they say springs eternal but I say
hope is solid, factive
it is our all-season all-terrain our
home and native
shore

dawn is the land we thrive in, that's
our song its
theme, shored up here for something
we know nothing about
far out and away beyond.

Dawn
counts for a lot
with us, and accounts for a lot
or so I think I know —

SHORELINE

Ashes to ashes, snow to snow.
The ash is a species threatened by the emerald ash borer.
Ottawa is soon to be denuded of trees by 50%. Ash-bound ourselves
we are 'bracing for massive destruction of forests in Ontario and Québec
  in the next fifteen years.'

Imagine this shoreline without Isolde
      Imogen
    Morgan and
  Beatrice   Tristan
       Anselm
          Seraphim and Gregory
home-brew christenings for ash trees whose arabesques chisel mosaic chips
  into the cloisonné of sky against the bit of *fleuve* we call home.

How do without? How *not* this
    mosaic air on a G string, this gut-bark and blank?
  its seeds of snow horizontal on the vector of wind
orient express pit-stopped by ash? this *kind* of
morning light 'new every morning' with 'the love our wakening
    and uprising prove'?
What has Love got to do with it
    the blinking out of another of Love's species?
Did he who made the lamb make thee? Or did *we* make the emerald threat?

The maker of alle thing
sees with a bigger scan than I can pretend to.
Take off your sandals, this is holy ground.

The Church is its members future and past, with the present :
    the communion of saints.
The Earth is its members future and past, with the present :
    the communion of species.

Does the Head of the Body have a choice? Or does he,
      did he, give it to us?
Is it something we said? We apologize.

Where do we sit at ease — if ease is allowed — in the present; where
      is the still small voice, the true north of this turning, this
          world, your cell that teaches you everything?
How put the rest back into the rest of it? Bared of limbs
whose amputation from Love's body bares our souls' grievance, how
         best comport the limbs left us?
      How bear it
unbearing them?

What you don't know does hurt you.
Imagine knowing.
Imagine denominations of trees, confessions of mammals
          covenants of birds and
        sects of lost insects, vestigial limbs of Church
     withering joyfully away
that they may be One.

The scientific writing's on the wall ready for dream analysis :
this is not forever. Ashes to ashes.

     Thou thy worldly task hast done,
     Home art gone, and ta'en thy wages;
     Golden lads and lasses must
     As chimney sweepers come to dust.

When God shall be all in all, it is *home* that we'll be — ash and all.
Imagine knowing that.

'I REPEAT MYSELF'

'I repeat myself'
says the sun
boring his audience with yet another

rise, another up, another
new, fresh, another
chance, another certain sure.

Tautology, redundancy :
there are things
not smiled upon

in business or
grammar or poetry.
Or poetry?

We don't say
the same thing
over and over?

You don't say.
Tell me another.
The wallpaper

of our lives is just one darn
novelty after another.
Shall we agree

to accept
pattern for pattern, up for up for up,
salute the drop drop drop this

endless wearing of us
down to down to
down to nothing is?

Poetry
sun
repeating.

IN THE GLOAMING

If you're on the north shore
you face south.
You're a sunrise people.

Others will have to hymn the sunset; the best we can do is
our *Phos hilaron* as light's shadows crumple, falling from
the hump-backed frozen waves before our sunrise eyes, definition lost
to the brush of twilight from this shore to far shore
to those southerners who face north.

Nightfall and the snow is clean erased, *tabula*
almost *rasa* before the… uh, onset of the
        fearful green
of the neighbour's sick glare, his
garage lamp! — joyless *carnaval* against the bogey dark
to chase away… what? Mutinous deer?
Piratizing porcupine?
A skunk *à l'école buissonnière*?
Our woods' creatures,
        his green glare.

We go to bed at eight now of a night :

        Nothing of us that doth fade
        but doth suffer a *fleuve*-change
        into something rich and strange

into a people that sleep and wake
with spring of day
who once began work when the midnight telephone stopped
and who now drop with the quick dark
        apart from
some star-gazing
some moon-gazing

some listening to the intense silence
>   some glaring of the green, the emerald threat
>   the evil eye.
Some glaring *at* it, exchanging hexes.

Snow's complicit with sun, snow's sun's hireling;
the shepherd has a stand-in, he can go off to the banquet
>   and the snow
will light us woollums with surrogate light all night,
stay us with second-hand sun.
>   Québec's gloaming.

Our eyes go roaming in the gloaming, feasting on the inhering light

>   …even the darkness is no darkness with thee,
>   but the night is as clear as the day:
>   the darkness and light to thee are both alike.

Green has its place.
Thumbs, frogs, lily pads, croquet hoops, lawn clippings, tea, old
orange peels on the compost heap, tall lime drinks, banking cooperatives,
jewellers' visors, zippers, old leather tomes, old study lamps, Copenhagen
copper rooves, carpets in bedrooms, sheets with William Morris willow
pattern, willows, elms, ginkos, gooseberries, leeks, pipsissewa,
unripe apples on the tree, ripe pistachios peeking out of their shells,
rotten mussels not peeking out of theirs, absinthe, beer
in a Québec pub on St-Patrick's Day,
these have their place in the scheme of green.

But Not Green Glare On Snow
on pristine white unlit or moonlit or shepherd-lit or hireling-lit
black-light-lit *snow!*

Snow is white.
Chameleonesque blue or mauve, or grey, or gold maybe. Not green.
Under it is green. *Over* green is *white.*
Let's get this right.

PEOPLE WHO LIVE

People who live in glass houses
sunbathe.

Once the seal on the day's package slit,
sun pops, light squirts, ultraviolet leaks, and the skin
begins its melanomic countdown.
Our days are numbered in suns and spots. It's skin and sun
all the way, till death us do part.

This light we die of
it offers us a dying into more light.
Is that the Way and the Truth?
I am the Way, the Truth and by the way the Death?

We're reluctant to condone suicide, hang on! we say,
lâche pas! Yet we lie in the sun.

I fall asleep in a cloud of unknowing, the sun bright on the bed
                                through a dozen glass panes
                        basking in the Presence…
            the Bridegroom in the midst of his swift course
riding his chariot up the skies, loving his creation.
                This is *the* contemplative fix, *voyons!*
to bask in the Son is the very model of contemplative prayer.

                And gradually
the sun changes your skin, your borderland and *doucement*
we are divinized 'until our singeing day' when

what else? we fall asleep in the Sun.

THE RAISED EYEBROW

So the moment :
you
like any Cro-Magnon throwing his
femur into the air in *2001: A Space Odyssey*

as the brass chords of 'Thus Spake Zarathustra'
ta-da-dah!... upwards and
up comes the citation, the golden eyebrow :
'And I quote'.

That raised eyebrow questions the horizon.
There it is : the moment you wait for, hope for, cheer for.
The eye is nothing compared to the eyebrow.
You'll see, it will get smaller and smaller

that eye up there in the blue yonder
eyebrows singed to nothing.
But the citation begins, here
at the horizon, eyebrow on its face.

(Well, where else would you expect an eyebrow?
Except perhaps you'd expect
the citation mark to be standing
like a sentence, a pronouncement.

Well, but the sun, the horizon, the earth.
You are prone too, to watch.)

It says of the day, the earth, 'And I quote'.
And what follows is of course
the citation, the day, the earth,
the living of it.

At the other side of earth
in the course of things comes 'End of quote'.
A golden fauve-red eyebrow
sinks from sight. But that's beyond our reaches.

We're a sunrise people.
Here we only start to speak.
And that's the story
of when sight is cited.

TRANSFIGURATION

'Lord, it is good for us to be here.' Peter
not such an ass with that, you know.
Many a true word spoken in mist… the Cloud
coming on, the unknowing.
      The building of houses, that's
what's on trial.

The *fleuve* is blue as Welsh slate this morning,
      as labradorite,
ram between two rods of ice, the maple sap suspended mid-run
        a Sanko Line freighter
      green as a glacier
sliding down to sea.

To build or not to build, before the transfiguring lightrise
coram Deo in a house, new every morning and only ever once.
We are a building species, we're Doozers. We *do*.
Sometimes the right building doesn't happen.
But the instinct's a grace, human, along
      with swallows, beavers, bees :
      Stonehenge and Poustinia,
        Kelmscott, Little Gidding,
          Sylvanès, Snowmass.
A house to share with God, a house to cohabit where
two worlds mesh : wick to the eternal.

Roof.
Each man beneath his own — vine and fig tree encumbering the eaves.
Chimneypots of offering up.

The house is an incarnation, brooded over by the Engendering One.
All house is flesh, *la chair* from which we speak, deliver,
sing, praise, gasp, laugh, *voyons!* 'the purpose
of the Christian life is the acquisition of'
      the capacity to say
'Lord, it is good for us to be here.'

The roofing act is a sacrament of lodging, abiding
in Edenland. 'If you wish, I will make three dwellings'.
We dwell here 'home' for a bit
and our mode of 'here' is house,
        is tent, is ark, shack, booth.
        If we're lucky.
Blessèd are they who can repeat after me 'it is good for us to be here' in
their magnified cell, magnifying. Flying on Nyssa's 'wing' by standing still.
Remaining is an entertainment of stability.
'Here I will sit and rest awhile:/ under...'.

               In
          under
      watching the riverbreath
'joy, the best of all our knowing' — God in our mist : Emmanuel.

Peter's instinct was enduranceward.
But the transfiguration passed, God in the mist when
        suddenly
there was 'no one with them any more, but only Jesus'.
'Only' indeed!
The cloud arrived, cooled things off, muffled up a silence.
Only ever once.

Look, if we could sustain the transfiguration we could drink the cup.
Zebedee's kids knew less what they were saying
than Peter 'not knowing what he said'.

And stilled
        it is good for us to be here.

LENTEN ARRAY

'Thou, dear child of Mary,
art the refined molten metal of our forge.'
Gloze of some old 15th century Irish sinner with perfect pitch.

Poured ladleful of molten copper
a dropped disc held whole by meniscus on the cusp of the *rive sud*
where the strait goes bent.
One dawn among many.

'Christ the fair glory' one dawn among many.
Flesh in clothes aflame and flaying in first degree,
mortal agony.
Hammerwork on the horizon of humus-land
our home and native. Corners of the map :
        here be sons and daughters
           made of flesh and pain.
         Here be our forge
       where God is anvilled human.
    No : where human is hammered divine.
  Which?

The disc burns silver on a sky *argent* — mere minutes later.
Gone the fair glory,
now the fair stirling *absconditus* :
    we are hid with Christ in scrim.
        After a vacation the river
      sighs mist again, transient, semiscient
    in the *fleuve* of the omniscient.
Molten silver on a forge of steel.

That too passes.

Cornsilk sun in a shell-blue sky.
One day among many.
Daily table on which we are pummeled fit for keeping kingdom's company.

'Go to your cell; your cell will teach you everything.'
From my everything, day by day like daily bread I watch
the mortar-and-pestle work of the Sun,
                              see myself milled, 'kned',
                    soldered into shape,
              filed, torqued,
          seeing-eye flesh cell by cell holified if I can but let the heel of his palm
          press and his arm strike.
This is the killing ground. This is where things die.

It is Ash Wednesday. The left-over ash
of argent sky is littered about my feet, still smouldering.
My body is burnt with divine.
It must have felt something like this, leaping to earth in a blaze of will,
comet of Bethlehem
ready to be clobbered to a spike of mortality.
                    If we go the other way
              we pass the same strait gone bent.
We straiten.

This is the healing ground, sun burning
on a ground argent : cautery,
angel to the lips of Isaiah. Your cell
will teach you everything : wisdom of a desert solitary.
Each bodily cell's a fractal of this fastness that teaches; your cells
                    will teach you everything
              all about devastation.
          You are ash, and to gold you shall return
panhandled alchemy of daily Sun.

Lenten fast, healing ground,
              cell to cell, magma to metal :
          for the *soi-disant* 'king's evil', King's welling touch,
Sun's soul's cure.

Lent I : In the blink

It's a secret, sunrise.
You thought it was self-evident. You stood before it
seeing the light break, what's to wonder?

But broken! — how?

'In the twinkling of an eye' he'd said
stammering the mystery
that will out.

Here's for all beginnings.
Again. Do we suffer to see change? — even
'something rich and strange'. *Och!* shreds of runes.

Was that you who winked?
Here's 'for all the saints
who from their labours…'.

A tinker tinkers; a saint saints.
'If it ain't broke'… but it is.
'Who from their labours wrest…'

(snatch-tunes snatch-
tunes) angels who quit at dawn
all-kindly. Or was it you who quit.

Are we enjoying ourselves yet?
'that the body you have broken may rejoice.'
('We shall all be changed' — pass it on.)

When the light breaks, when the light returns,
its many happy returns, when the light's
direct, inaccessibly direct in Light inaccessible,

when the Light's unbearably light
when the Weight's unbearably weighty
you shut it out.

Broken Light.
Each blink fractures it, each mini-inattention.
Reception is everything.

No. It is nothing.
Guilty bystander doesn't change original accident.
Does. Reception : the readiness is all — he wrote.

Thread upon thread of strings of minutest inattentions,
that's the eye for you,
the brain, the heart's valves.

What did you want : the whole thing coherent?
And unending? Sunrise
without the high noon shoot-out?

Just sunrise, and sunrise, and sunrise,
without a single blink? Could you?
Could you bear it?

That's the secret.

LENT II: I'VE DONE IT AGAIN! SAYS THE SUN

The ephemera are tooling upstream today : *glissade* —
    passengers in an airport between terminals
        standing the moving walkway
            leaning into their leaving.
Tracks of a far animal — deer?
the neat red fox? a bird? a ghost? — cross clean across
the blank snow from the rock beach-steps
    to the apple tree, then leave…
        sheer   blank

like the time the murdered female pine grosbeak disappeared from the
        drift… after
five feet away, a pair of prints landed
            step, step
        by webbed step, into the   blank
            to where the grosbeak left its angel-in-the-snow and then —
and since — nothing.
Murdered by a transparent pane of glass she was.
Eaten by a fellow flyer.
'Out, out, brief flight'… signifying
    nothing.

A freighter passes upstream.
A freighter? — nothing but a skeleton
    skinny mechanical innards all on show
        low in the mist, a blueprint for a boat
           diaphragm without song.   Gone.

The helicopter came and went, everything's upstream on the horizontal
today, only the sun does vertical
crossing this criss on a coriolis slant, inveterate.
    I've done it again! says the sun.
There are rules….

The passengers have made their flights by now, under sun's rule, nothing
but the river now, and the Watchers and the Holy Ones.
Where are they?
                        Step, step
               by triune step
and gone.

My language can't decline a river like *'fleuve'* and *'rivière'*.
It takes being here
to know and say what goes all the way Grand Trunk to
join the all-in-all, direct current.
The ephemera *du jour* fly upstream
                   but the direction
          is down,
the undertow asserts the law. Time and tide are *copie conforme*.

'Yet a little while', tide comes in on this fluvial channel.
By Trois-Rivières no tide is perceived, but here — tidal freshwater
new every morning.
          We are half-way
               here
                     between saltwater tide and no tide
                             on the noble deacon's noble *fleuve*.
The empire is dying
             but Holy Laurent still rallies the poor
                     to heap coals on the heads of the GOP.
We watch it on television every night these days. How long will it last?
I've done it again! says the sun. Yet a little while.

But there are laws, you know that, sunny.
What goes up must come down. Forget all my Ascension Day sermons on
what comes down must go up.
This one's headed for perdition. The ephemera score again.

So hang onto the *fleuve*
               by fistfuls. It's going all the way
          all the way
       to nowhere
All in All.

LENT III : OCHON OCHRIE

There is no colour at all this morning. It's an old archival sepia photograph of the *Anse de Portneuf*. Or it's a Tony Hauser silver print, or platinum-coated 'heirloom', *imago Dei*, portrait of the artist as a landscape.

The artist is not the photographer. The photographer looks, bears witness, 'I am a camera', testifies : here is God's face from this *belvédère*. 'I am a seagull! No, that's not it.'

There is no colour this morning. 'Cry, the Beloved…'. How snatches of cadences whirr by, *'Ochon, ochon, ochrie!'*, scraps of detritus that were someone else's treasures. 'I am a camera!'

What heirloom shall we leave from this *anse*? Snatches of anger… why such anger from this perch *expectans*? — what some call purgatory. Anger won't settle for despair or joy, insists on occupying the middle ground.

There is — unexpectantly? — one red roof way far on the far shore. Suddenly in the platinum, a roof-red roof. A no-name shorebird passes overhead. *'Ceci n'est pas une* seagull'.

The letter A is red. *Anse* begins with it, and Appetite, and so does Anger. But not *colère*; *colère* is almost *couleur*, which is almost *couleuvre*. 'I wish you joy of the worm.' No, that's not it.

Ecclesia expectans is another version of social suffering. But they call it *penitens*. Wrong. If you've got to *penitens* you've got to joy. You doubt? 'I only am escaped alone to tell you'. Portrait of the artist.

Did you know that suffering was expectant? Have you any idea how much the women of Congo *hope*? Have you any idea how much they *love* through it all? *Tendresse*, care and anguish for the raped three-year-old itself the child of rape, *did you hear me,* one of the many the mother-body submitted to, what choice, going on mothering because the submission is to *something else.*

A is for *Amour*. We have to settle for 'Love'; it's not said with the lips the same. (Pause.) We *have* to settle for Love, to *settle* Love. Love is the settlement. There is no colour at all this morning, but a red roof

and the cliffs stark sharp *noir-et-blanc* as if lit from within, as if there is no light in the air today, all light banked up within, as you bank a fire, as you bank your treasure, someone else's heirloom. Or detritus, someone else's life going to waste with your own.

We require this purgatory, this expectancy. Love's settlement's outpost. And the light is banked, boxed, x-ray-penetrant. Light from Light. *Something else.*

LAETARE

There is no rose of sych virtu
    as was the Son this dawning through
a crack of cloud, such solid slabs
    of slate like millstones over and
below the rose there blooming to be ground to grey.

Nothing we eat from nature's growth
    is such a hue : a rose indeed
without a trace of gold, sheer rose
    and hewn head and toe into a
thick flat bowl — a poppy? no
a rose — in the act of being decimated by the world's tectonic plates.

Minutes later, brief life, the rose is gone, ground, grey, but wait,
there later yet's this glorious arising
    which rose over the upper plate of killing slate a golden radiance,
        an ahhh!
Ah but. Minutes later, brief Emmaus, all is grey
and this world has reassumed its eyeless theocalypse.
    There is no eye, of sych virtu.

That's as far as this dawn got. I report it to you.
The people that walked in darkness saw a great light.
The people that walked after saw the embers, and the best of them became
pokers and bellows for the rest of us. But wait… the breath.
There was given the breath. *Ha!*
        the Pentecostal gift as a set of bellows, a *soufflet*
          huffing on the coals
       till we can heap them
    living fire on folks' heads :
love's revenge.

Mary has to sit out the sunrise. It's about her son. Sorry, Mary,
you can watch, with us.

There is no eye of sych virtu
    as was the eye of Mary who
'saw heaven and earth in lytle space'

running about her kitchen. That's the eye we train, beachcombers
riddling our grey for gold, and look, there it is, *terre*
shot through with *ciel, glaise* with glint. *Lux.*

The grey panoply of this early morning, post-rising
is the effect of water on the earth's fabric
                the circular *virtu*
    of river to air to cloud
to snow to river. Earth's silk is *moiré.*

Living water wields its warp and we are engraved with gleam.
'Blessed are those who have not seen and yet believe'; yeah, yeah
        but it's *here*
            in the wonder of the world
                that you let drop your glove, O hidden one flashing
            O designer with your luxurious fabrics come buy
        without money and without price.
Lux in mundo.

    There is no rose, no gold, no grey, of sych virtu
        as is the world of every day and every hue.

LENT V : BYSTANDER AT A SUICIDE

Give us this day our daily disc.
We're all gathered here, the invitees :
the upright trees, the recumbent posturers in their privileged bed
the tiny voles with their no-footprints

the invisible quick red fox, even
the lazy yellow dog (somewhere — the nosey one who zig-zagged our turf)
waiting for our host.

And he comes, a perfect pancake flaming from the oven, too hot
to eat but we have several choruses to go before the tongue'll hit the taste,
we can wait. We have always waited.

Each day's waiting is broken only by restless sleep.
Even sleep knows it's waiting. Will *this* be the day? Oh, whence for me
shall my solution come, from whence arise?

Yet each day we do receive our daily disc.
Sometimes behind the humeral veil, no matter, we gazers know, we think,
that it's there receiving us : our host. Except that
we're receiving it. Him. You.

If you are Love coming out of 'that depth around all things and beyond all
things' with transformations for me in your pockets, if you are this Person
the holy one says you are
why am I bereft?

I've had my daily viaticum but the journey doesn't happen.
You know what stuck is? You never were.
What's unassumed is unhealed, you know they say. Is there to be no end to
this waiting?

Watching the last breaths of the dying grosbeak still brings mourning
to my eyes. Three little sighs
she gave, poor love, and went still, there in the snow.

She never knew what struck her it was over that fast.
One minute joy on the wing, then…. No, that's not it.
'I am a grosbeak!'

Have you joy on the wing for me in your stash? A little kingdom fodder?
Haven't we got things the wrong way round? the old? I pine.
I'm still in the snow, frozen. When's the flight?
What is this, Psalm 88?

The redpolls lark about in the sunrise, comical, entertaining —
sepia-tint birds with one roof-red cap like bellhops.
They jostle seeds on the dead coneflowers.

Entertaining is receiving,
the step or flight I cannot take
for all my eyes are bigger than my stomach.

Unto the *fleuve* around do I lift up my longing. Is that it?
No, not it. Fall of a sparrow.
New every morning is the dark night of the soul.
And yet we feast. And yet we feast.
Bystander at a suicide. One Corinthians eleven, twenty-nine.

FFRAED'S-LIGHT

Ffraed's-light, Ides-light
    around these Ides, this Ides, 'Ides'
        like 'sheep' both singular and flocking
            one or many naming the turn of the season
with its lamb-drop milk let-down : *Imbolc*.
And the tending.
Ffraed's forearms, midwife to middlemarch
      'dipping first one hand, then two hands, freeing the river to flow'
        tending the *sanctuaire*, easing the birth.
           Forearms in the birth canal.

She strode by,
the Wisdom Bride, Brigid, Ffraed
a while ago, the Kalends of her feast-month, her *gwyl*
    she strode across our frozen land
        waking my husband from sleep, silently.
This is my day, she didn't say.
Black as a crow she was and wore.
    Shins white.
        Left to right and gone.

The thaw abroad in our land. Sun's
behind it all. The veil of Moses.
The first two turtledoves, under the lovers' window : there
where heat of home meets downdrift
a sand walkway for their graces. *His* work, *his* wonder.

Two black crows begin to stake claim. I must rethink crows.
I must rethink bereavement.
      'Ffraed is come. Ffraed is welcome'.
        The song of the turtle, mourning dove's appoggiatura
    on a spring tonic.

The Spirit-season of winter white, oh
   the high holy hovering season 'with ah! bright wings'
    I am bereft of, yes.
Because yes, the Spirit points away from itself, always.
    Lets Ffraed.

Lets Ffraed deliver
   dipping first one forearm, then two forearms
    freeing the *fleuve* to flow into time of earth
     time of soil, time of body.

The inner work is done, it is 'weldone'. Welcome.
Expect nothing.

Unstuck. Ffraed is the meaning of unstuck.
White is the meaning of the Spirit.
   Snow, milk, wool, bleach, the biblical radiances. The Mercy.
Shins and forearms white, here on sacred shores
   striding from left to right, blessing in time of thaw
    blessing the channel's rush, melted edge rushing at us as it
   rushes left, downstream to the mother-lode.
The veil of black Bride, cover against *his* radiance.

He's coming.
Why does the Resurrection
   seem so much like the Incarnation?
A second coming.

At the Equinox the *rayon vert* will shine
through the foot of Jesse onto the *chaire* or *chair* of Christ
in the *cathédrale de Strasbourg*. Then, and in fall.
We'll see.
Expect nothing. For now
the Holy Ones are gathering, the *rayon vert* is in the wings, waiting, then
   it's onto the holy stage from left to right and on.
    On into time of black seed
     time of white flow.

TWIG SUNDAY

The bully birds are criss-crossing our space
        crow's-cradle of pathways
slooped in the air strung between trees.
The game begins at dawn.

Doozers, these crows.
One bounces on a branch till it breaks
'won't hold no nest that one'; tries another;
eyes the farther-ups; later, jousts twigs from their limbs
        flies off triumphant :
raven with a dove's sign of dry land in his beak
        to build, to build.

The avant-garde of Canada geese
are canadianing it around, not much talking, not much strutting
but game for a joyride on the ice floes
let the tide do the work   up
      back

        up
     back   their mercy-go-round on one plane.
Some of them pass the night on the water among the floes, head
tucked into wingpit, at ease among the jostlings of ice :
fleuve, 'where geese may safely snooze'.
They safely graze too, at low tide, on our beach, the roots of rushes.

Do they feel watched over? Knowingly *coram Deo*
repentant tax collectors quitting the temple at peace having shat out the
        week's sins? Do they feel
      'judged yet not turned away'? Do they know
    they belong — and oh! they belong, these *Canadiens errants* —
part of the icon of God, freckles on the face
of the earth which is the face in God's mirror?

Oh Luv, your beauty leaves me breathless.
What's a poor lung to do, heigh nonny
but holler up a storm of assent — as if assent could speak
        as if assent were anything more than holding here
            on a sit-stay
      heels, haunches, chin, crown, hock, tail, wingblade
        being your
    creature, alongsider of the *bernache du Canada*
      wreath-crowned with
your glory while the tide at its 'long, withdrawing roar, retreating…
down the vast edges… and naked shingles of the world'
    speaks not to a nonsense born of a darkling plain but
      to sense — a makessense of All Sorts.

How the heart heaves to an optimism in despite of all, of
September 11th, of Zimbabwe, Sudan.
How the heart's fire is *a priori*, a non-negotiable
    sense at the root of things will-ye nill-ye.
Meaning is not ours to make or break, the job's been done;
    just bide   the tide
       tide in
         tide out
   its sevenfold *is*, true, and God's and
accomplished in despite of darkening pain
     in respite of Job's grief, given.

Cross before me, cross beside me
   behind at point of sunset
     over
      under
       and in sunrise;
          he must have known this even as he groaned
      before Lazarus's tomb
    grieving at the job to do
   foreseeing Veronica, and
Mary   with
  the other
   son.

SEEING THROUGH HOLY WEEK

When Christ is 'outed'
when his depths of divinity are let show
the disciples see through, look through, they *do* 'through'
before the empowering disempowering depth.

And they fall. We all fall down.
Hush-a, hush-a! — 'falling' in every direction, with every sense.
We fall from those heights, scudding off crags good enough for holding
       blessèd Moses, blessèd Elijah, the visionaries, the Companions.
Were they in the desert with him, too?
      On either side the cross?
           (Have they made it up with Paul? Rude about the veil, he was.)

But it is free fall, liberated fall, for us, *les délivrés* : what it is
for human mortals to be slain weightless in the Spirit
      into the depths
          into the waters of his company.
We fall through the looking glass, like Alice, and there's another world
      the same world other :
the icon as window as icon.

And now this window : its turn.
This icon of *les oies des neiges*, many snows, multiple geese.

'Who are these robed in white?' (in good biblical conformity)
'Who are these in dazzling brightness?' (hymnalfuls of)
      whelming with their radiant whiteness
          witness
      clouds of
     wheeling in air
    taking your breath away with the glory :
nature transfigured — that is, as it has always been.

As it is, in its depths. The window an icon and there, see,
the body of the Holy One flanked by his rooted saints
      in all their branchedness and budding,
          the Watchers.
      Stable in their hospitality, they shall crowd into a shade :
outed mustard seeds and kingdom come.

'The human mortals want their winter here;/ No night
      is now with hymn or carol'; the high Holy
Spirit-season robed in white's been put on hold.
But the geese, the geese swing Spirit to spring
      itinerant wing upon wing
          they *out* the depths of the glory —
              though they do nowt but float in giant goose-booms
        like *les raftmans* and their logs moving downriver
      or like ice-floes *redivivi* in the spring channel
or though they seem merely to wheel in formation in the air
        high-wire liturgists.

Theirs is the great tattoo, the divine in mortal dosage, theirs
      is the open secret parading before your eyes
        iconic in the wet
      in the waters of his company :
le fleuve, there for the outing.

Until the evil one in his acid seaplane sprays from his fly-over
and again
and again
until Man has reconfigured the word 'dominion' to his liking.

One last sunrise

Between Gethsemane by dark and Calvary by day, he drank the cup. One last sunrise for the Son of Man. One last swaddling of the east in bands of rose, gold, peach — then perfect day. One last sun of his many suns, of the many moons he knew, the 34 winters, the 33½ springs. Then the laying in the tomb like a manger.

As the sun shone, before the veil of the temple was rent and the clouds or was it eclipse effaced the face, the fair glory uttered the flint-fair words we hum and humble at, puzzle out, try to rumble as the earth rumbled its dead that day, disgorging saints.
And Christ rumbled hell.

Holy Saturday was a hell of a busy day. Moling it down under. And *then* for all those roads *above* ground! the trekking, rallying, sign language, exhortation. And oh yes, the good food. Eats to be had at The Sign of the Fish.

But before all that, the cup. Held twice, so some said, at the Sign of the Upper Room, before the meal and after the meal, the cup shared. But that's not it. It's the cup not shared, a cup only ever on this earth once perhaps, who knows, who knew, the cup the Zebedee boys don't drink. Peter neither. Not *this*. The cup by dark he prays let pass.
But it doesn't.

'Why have you forsaken me?' Some suspect that that was all. The hard edge of the bespoke Saviour. Some affect that he soft-soaped it : forgive, commend, paradise. But the cup, that cup he'd dreaded in Gethsemane, pondered before the tomb of Lazarus, that iron chalice now he seized in both spike-driven hands.
'I am thirsty!'

The finish-line is in sight, 'Let me go there' is done, has been; he went, he came, the great lark of exaltation down, passed the humus test, good earth of humiliation, now for bronze, irony-clad and exaltation regained, from wood he would reign Mercy; he is ready to drink Gethsemane, eager to drink Gethsemane, this is his Coventry his not-there looming, his thirst at the well, welcoming the woman, her good wood bucket. *Yes.* I can drink it. I *will* to drink it. (The cup the Dayspring'd prayed let be.) 'I am *thirsty*' for it.

Then, 'It is finished.' Gold! The Personal Saviour's Personal Best, the last kick and the Glory's nailed. *Yes!*   Blackout.   Come the rhythms of recognition, the transfiguring body they could never hold a roof over, the mystic barbecue, the Cloud. Sign. Sign.
Sealed. Delivered.

EASTER MORNING

Running from the tomb.
You could say that of all of us.
How sunrise casts the tomb's vacancy

out along the pebble road our feet
fly over, never mind the blisters, never mind
the labouring lungs

this is news, this beats Chicken Little, the Sun is fixed,
the rise is Perpetua's milky joy and
Felicitas birthing in prison before the wild beasts' breakfast

is Perpetual we would say, Sun
caught in the shutter speed
for all time from without beginning

the Rising.
This is what we have been trying to say in our awkward way
to all our lovelies : You *can* bear it

birthing our joys. 'Are we there yet?'
Oh, kids…! (sidelong love, aseat aside). Yes
dears, yes we are there yet.

The sun is rising.
Time to up
and run.

THE EIGHTH DAY

It would look like this
the redeemed world
sun just
up

It would look like this
water seeking its level
shore just
by

It would look like this
the 'perpetuity'
only just
'in'

It would look just like this
air meaning music
earth

meaning hearth meaning heart
stone meaning precious
owned

only
without price.

It would look like this
precisely.

The hermit at sunrise

Alone's impossible, the air is filled with effluvia,
divine's issue. The Living One's its show and tell, its Child at play —
        or the Living One's alter ego is, his Other I who AM
on earth even as I IS in heaven.

Give us this day. *Yes!*
Each grackle sheen and starling joke of it, each
white-crowned bald-eagled boondoggle,
        bring it on!
The hermit doing sunrise on the mean altar of his ego.

Hermit at sunrise
        wing-watching, cousined with wings.
Haloes of flight. How
the Alter One's so often shown with wings (alternate tongues).
Show and tell, Pentecost :
the bellows, the haloes, the windows onto, the tongues of, the Word for.

Alter ego *Ecce Spiritus* by water and by blood, bearing witness.
John's way of seeing,
        truthing
        by river and by mortal.
Merton alone, to write so as to love.

Zen in, Zen out, the great judo-breath of the river
        tide in
                tide out
        slow as time : time's open secret   breath in
breath out   the shore the Spirit's diaphragm, its long slow blink
        of breath in
                tide out
        tide in
breath out   in river rune in   in Word out :
        the unimaginable immanence codified
                        codex in short-hand.
The world is God's short-hand.

Still, stiller, stillest : the invisible tide.
(Not like last night, when the boat's wake on the low mudflats
                        sent ranks of white breakers at breakneck
                speed surfing to shore
           band upon band of ribbon of wet
      the length of the coast.
A good five minutes.)

This can't keep up.
Slowness rushes by into day.
And on. Gave us this day.

Gave us this morning, sunrise
the Ghost in the levee.
Did give.
Kingdom come.

Harvest home : Ascension Day's first fruits returning with evidence
from off-shore —
testimony of the untouchables from the Untouchable :
how the altar of the ego's made of muscle —
       diaphragm capable of sighing (flames)
           'it *can* be done'
      you can get there from here.
Give us that day

'...hiding these things from the learned and wise...
      revealing them to the simple.'
           On this altar. *Le moi brûlé.*

That day when
      we shall be lightwardly lofted
         wing-lit and -light :
           what it is to
bare one's witness to the wind, give the sole breath up to it
      breathing in sunrise
breathing out day. Over. Up. Over and
out. Kingdom home.

THE SWAN AT SUNRISE

Why am I so sure it was a 'he'?
A kid, a youth just reaching swanhood alone among the geese
        floating at sunrise surrounded by aliens.
Proof text : this 'teen', this 'ado' was
imprinted to his own kind, classic, and he
called off and on with one, light, plaintive toot (a grown-up peep)
calling for his own, his lost.

Long neck straight as a croquet mallet, its buff hue
of almost-maturity and he alone, not in his gang.
        Snow geese all round
        clubby and content and coherent;
lone whistling swan, beeping.

And why has my heart broken for him?
Why so forlorn, my soul?
Would he have coped better as a girl,
is it a guy thing to be rudderless without the game team
        the grid of rules
        the binary logic?
Does it matter.
The sorrow's for the isolation,
effort of communication falling on deaf ears, bewilderment :
'Why am I not answered? Why me? Not 'us'?'

Geese answer incessantly.
Come dusk as I sit listening to the resident shoreline orchestra
tuning

                              and up,
               and up,
     up,

                              white with piety
                  maestro Dark about to appear
            and then all goose heaven'll break out as they
        lob their polyphonies full-shout till day
I plaint : 'Why so forlorn, O my soul?'

At sunrise the swan, wingspan of a grown man, had moved on upstream
and what becomes of him who knows. The will to solitude
among the solitaries is pungent, desert-strong.
But a swan?

The poet in the crowd whom no one reads, his words
'tortuous' says the unreader and tosses them away
                          unwrung…
              so much swansong
        malign detritus…
that threatens solitude with incoherence. It aches the heart.

Three white-crowned sparrows prepare for maestro Dusk
with collations of bugs from our soil
not bothered by my presence.
They signal their collusion with a high-pitched
        'tzip' — communicant with each other. Of each other.

Being a communicant has this other sense : participation
as a transitive verb. Not only
do we communicate Love's body, the bread and the wine
(or the bug and the soil), we 'participate' love,
    not just *in* love.
        Though 'in love', too.
And a transitive ache is its antinomy.

One swan at sunrise.

We can't do it alone : life. I'm not doing this alone.

THE CROW AT SUNRISE

Craw! sixteen times.
Craaww! twenty-seven times.
Craaawww! fifty-one times. A'right a'ready, I'm awake.
Crow unstoppable. Caughghgh!! There's spring for you. Mating season.

> Three craws sat upon a wa',
> Sat upon a wa', sat upon a wa'.
> Three craws sat upon a wa',
>> On a cauld and frosty mornin'.

Female as possession. Vaunt it, screw the lot of them then brag about it.
    Uh-huh. Crows : gulling it in the rushy shallows.
Black posing as white. Bullying the littoral.

> The first craw fell and broke his jaw,
> Fell and broke his jaw, fell and broke his jaw.

I wish. *That* would be a good Aesop fable.

> The first craw fell and broke his jaw,
>> On a mild and misty mornin'.

    We've *had* one hatch,
how many more cacophonies do the natives have to submit to
    here at *fleuve*-side?
Moi-moi-moi-moi-moi! Yeah! Yeah! Yeah! says Sir Crow thirty-four times more.

    Doesn't she settle, *la dame*?
Why is this one purring in that wheedling way,
    the Lady is a tramp?
Are crowesses cats with nine mates?

Quai-quai-quai! caws Sir Crow. Cruck, crrruck, crrrruck, coos the Lady
rhyming with *hang on* a mo :
> there on our rock-wall shoreline, chummy in black
> isn't that
feeding I just saw? Is *that* the Lady — on the *right*?
On the *left* is that a big fat juvenile son-of-a?

The inside of his beak shows pink like a puppy's — *crrruhhg??*
> submissive wheedling, the beak, open, points *up*
> though he's big as a boy scout leader
> she no bigger. Up, for food to be put in.
She does.
Well, I'll be! From her beak to his. (I take note how I've assigned gender.)

> The second craw was greetin' for his maw,
> Greetin' for his maw, greetin' for his maw.
> The second craw was greetin' for his maw,
> > On a soft and summer mornin'.

Yet a while, weeks whiling away
and the big fat kid crow is still a dependent, needy
> of Mum's mercy; I've watched.
What is this, Down syndrome? can you have…?
Then one day I see. He's *lame*.

He's got one good leg to hop on, when he alights it's on his belly
> > and she
> she faithful
> she scavenges, she forages
she feeds
> he eats
> > she's skinny, they are almost inseparable.

Today, there on one of the flatter platterrocks, the pair sat
(his balance is wonky, he flops, he uses his wing as a crutch, a seal flipper)
> and she, loyal Lady Crow, her brood long gone
patiently
> voicelessly
> > does what must be done for her Tiny Tim.

Winter will come, dears. What will you do?
My paltry alms of bread and cheese and fish
cubed for your beaky dish,
serve you as I might, won't weather snowdrifts.

Black as my Tom's Brigid you are, wee Bridie full of grace,
little Mother of all the Rushes, and
black is the colour of your true love here.
I sing to you, my dear
you in your clericals
with your shower of mercy :

you show
how care and love
are cure of souls.
More than his.
More than yours.

The third craw, couldnae caw at a',
Couldnae caw at a', couldnae caw at a'.
The third craw, couldnae caw at a',
She was far too busy fetching.

THE HERON TEST

Dawn and
the herons' return.
Three four   six seven   eight!
    herons fly in from right
    to left
and cruise to a stand in our shallows,
take up their meditation.

So late this year! It's like a reprieve
a second first.
Let's hear it for contemplatives!

Once there were forty.
My near neighbour thinks
it's the presence of eagles that has scared them off.

What chance the contemplatives against the actives....

The time the bald eagle and the heron
shared a face-off on the rock
    on which
a fine large fish lay caught
who knows by whom — perhaps the gull
the one who left.
Couldn't stand the pressure.

The contemplative or the active :
who was going to get that fish?

There was a slow weighing of odds.
Twenty minutes maybe, those two
measured out each other's measure
shifted a muscle maybe an inch, maybe two, no more —
checked their weapons,
    gentlemanly Heron, all tall willowy nothing,
        squire Eagle, square block of power and sharp-eyed wit.

But Eagle *stood* on his weapons : those claws
while Heron's was ready-drawn : that rapier beak.
All this, their eyes and every fibre of each body measured
    the force of.
The true meaning of 'show-down'.

Finally, after a forever, the activist hunched up his shoulders
    spread his wings, gave up
        into the air and off.

Bless you, activist! Fair fly you, God speed you.
There is but one fish needful. Heron
has chosen the better part,
which will not be taken from her.

LITURGICAL COLOUR GREEN

A case of the vapours. 100% humidity
on the casement ajar so vapour can come and go
 like the cat.

Vapour, vapour everywhere nor any link to thought.
Sunrise behind seven veils
dew lines
 vapour trails
  8,000,000 succulent blinkering leaves
      rain   mist   cloud   air laden with riverbreath
        creekbreath streaking from creek to casement to far *cabanon*.

(The broken whites of the highway line
breathed up vapour in the headlights, did you notice?)

Brother Sun brothe vapour, hath brothen
 vapour by the veilyard this morning.
I haven't seen him rise in weeks. *Absconditus.*

I wear blinkers of succulent leaves
 the size of small boats :
rhubarb, zucchini, people ask what drug they're on, *tabernosh!*
They're on water, *taberouette*-wet-wet! intravenous.
The potato plants are falling over with water. Drunk.

My eyes breathe in river
 fleuve in   *fleuve* out
   tear-ducts   *ruisseau, ruisseau*   *eau de ruisse*

what is not river is almost-river
the green tidal-meadows rippling in the wind like wheat wet like green-
 waved water but it's reeds, *ruisses.*
Clouds lit with light of sun risen, it is risen indeed, alleluia.

None of this would be here but for Brother Sun, alleluia.
All of this would be burnt to a crisp but for Brother Sun his evaporizing
 Three All-kindly Absconditi.

The house is clicking in the heat, changing its size
   like a snake
finding its footing in the covenant of air, vapour of
   things hidden with the naked eye, seeing's nictitating blindness
the house changing shape under its no-gaze
   the wind full of wet : lymphatic system of the rivershore.
Sunlight glancing off....

(What) would I see without these eyes? — these water-logged globes
in a body 70% humidity in a climate 95% humidity, this moted 'I' balanced
   on the head of a pin whether to be air or river
water undecided whether to wet or to whisk, to sweat or to swale.
     (The woman born blind whose
   brain's recoded itself to receive
     sight from skin : the camera-trained tongue...)

'...because you have hidden these things from
the wise and intelligent and have revealed them'
   to the blind : light glances...
(play of peekaboo, the original and ultimate ...).

'You shall become like a watered garden, like a spring
whose waters fail not. And they who do these things
shall restore the wasted glories...'
     of All Sorts fallen for us
    who 'wait with eager longing...'

Little children, listen.
Bethany Mary, vertigo at the feet of Jesus
   not hearing for hearing. Hearing *through*.
Hear me through, hear through me :

the eyes obscure.
Look and 'look and not see', seeing *beyond*.

Something else.
Nor any thought to think.

OVER AND OVER

Over and over. Over and over
                the wallpaper of repeating prayer
as sun, as tide, as breath
                the rule of repeat, the :‖
    of the movement of earthen vessels into the day's flood
catch as catch can, come who may
without money and without price, come to the Pearl, come drink.

The tide comes in like the game behind the child's back,
how far can it creep unseen; I look, I look, and I never catch it at it
    yet the heron has had to abandon his rock.

Your cell, wallpaper of prayer, of
others' words, of stacked generations, piled plates of people preceding
silted down in time, middens of prayer
of this relation to Nature and we haven't even got to Other People.
        Just this
relation beaded on eyestrings, fishing-lines with their hooks invisible in
    the stealthy *fleuve* that creeps like the child behind the back
before the laughter, the burst of it
        and then
we do it again.

Our hooks into the flood of flow of what we can't catch at move but
which moves. In which we live and move. That one, you know the
    one I mean : and have our being.
That's the motif, the responsory, the collect, the snatch :
spirit of words past, Scrooge, sin, sorrow, song,
delight, desire, *délices* and we haven't got past Nature
        our abiding-place.

This is the first of the day. This is the opening paragraph
        the heron from his rock to ours
nearer, then with a *craaaq!* a burst of it, flies almost overhead.
(Inland? Why inland?)

I cast my eyehook back offshore
the north-east sun skipping its light at me, glancing off the *fleuve*
that steals (all stealth) towards my cell, our Pearl;
this is waterscape at play, this is Love at rest.
Over and over, over and over :
airscape, water- and landscape, fire, *feu, feu!* My joy, my joy!

Landscape is love
and those that abide in it abide in Love, and Love in them.

One thing have I asked of the Lord
one thing have I desired : even that I may dwell
in the scape which the Lord hath made all the days of my life,
to behold the fair beauty
and to seek him in this cell. Over and over.
Over and over.

These things will I remember
as I pour out my soul within me : one deep calleth to another
      flood to *fleuve*
eyestrings, Lord Spirit's seals, Donne's ecstasy. These
netting   strings are the unbreakable bonds of Love.
   hammocking

We are gathered up.

Madam's Canon : Riff on a folk-round

My dame hath a lame tame crow.
My dame hath a crow that is lame.
Ho! Let the slow crow go feed solo —
so shall he grow the same!

Whereas this river

Whereas this river
Whereas this place, including but not limited to its slice of flow
Whereas this slice of wind passing and raining mercy
Whereas this mercy
Whereas this piece of teeming life in and about the aforementioned river
Whereas this teeming with rain
Whereas this wetting
Whereas this mercy invisible to the naked eye;

Whereas the eye is not naked but veiled in cataracts
Whereas there is nothing to do but wait
Whereas the heron has landed and is looking down
Whereas the heron is stalking the fish
Whereas Christopher Smart went mad on the outside and sane on the in
Whereas neck and snake are cognate in a heron
Whereas there is nothing to do but wait at the void's edge
Whereas the quality of mercy is not strained
          but lumpy and unevenly distributed
Whereas this is the Seat;

Whereas this rain wouldn't drive anyone committed in
Whereas the heron just caught breakfast
Whereas contrabirdal woodland melodies from *gorges* invisible to the naked
          cataract are constituent of winged throats issuing alleluias
          from the edge of the grave or void
          or abyss, or gorge
Whereas the charism of a bird is wing and voice in alternating current
Whereas the river is similar and tidal
Whereas the Holy Spirit is similar though incommensurate and
          incommensurable

Whereas the Holy Spirit rushes in at the eye with all its voidal power
Whereas cataracts emulate the Cloud
Whereas that seems like a good idea
Whereas the Cloud is where it's at :

I, *La Recluse* of the *Mas du Refuge*, do hereby bequeath where it's at;

And moreover :
Whereas the disease infecting bloggers is a pandemic
        and the merciless blogger is driven in out of the reign for he wants
        no part of the mercy
Whereas he issues his instantial dicta like vomit and feels better after
Whereas winged internet and verbal disgorging make not a charism
        but pass for one in the virtual world
Whereas the invisible eye
Whereas the eye that sees into the heart of hearts
Whereas the invisual eye that rests upon Vaclav Havel and Barack Obama
        and Dag Hammarskjöld and Seraphim of Sarov is inscrutable
        to the naked blogger who is illiterate in Word
Whereas the Word is written in illegible red
Whereas the virtual bloggers are
        ineligible for the void for the mercy cannot host them
Whereas the abyss is mistakable for what it isn't;

Whereas there is nothing to do but wait;
Whereas the granite is imprinted with the flow of motions past
Whereas every bit of me but what's now is what's past :

I do hereby give, devise and bequeath the sunrise after the day I die
        and the sunrise after that
        and the nine after that
        and the twelfth, invisible to the naked eye
        and the thirteenth, visible to the Pearl
to the eyes in my stead that will 'aye' this flow for aye and
        a day hereinafter referred to as the Perpetuity;

And I bequeath my blind seers
    and my green thumbs
    and my heart's hole
        to the Perpetuity;

And I bequeath in Trust this piece of river, this peace
        of flow, this stationary motion, this winged stability
    this alternating current of
fire   water   air   cradle of rock   tide   berth of earth
            vantage edge
        cove
     flow

     vantage peace

   vantage   to do waiting with.
     nothing

AUBADES

Somewhere
  I read
Bertrand Russell
never didn't see a sunrise
  so he said.

He lived long.
  Aubades are health in song.

What about you,
        what about me?
How many did we miss, did we see,
on this short span we ran
  the same run as the sun?

If I were a doctor
I would treat my patients
  with sunrises.

  But for that
you'd need a different
meds plan
a different urbs plan…

  a different place
a different race.

BORN-AGAIN DAWN

Born-again dawn, Spirit licking at the lips of the trees does Truth
from still to stirred to still again.
Tiny Tim, carrion crow on his ash perch keeping the treatster
in view in her pine bed beside her flesh man.

Still-born dawn. The pok! pok! of guns. It's open season on ducks.
The two shore chairs lie keeled over in sympathy, possum hooves
in the air where the grass reaper passed.

(The grass rises and falls with mowing
like a tide. To-day's low : green velvet.)

The gunners in their keel-less tubs are pokking off the invisible ducks :
fairgrounds, a penny a pass.
Our ducks are wise,
they've cleared out. The decoys remain, virtual ducks, digital life.

In spirit and in truth (in holy writ). 'O Jerusalem, Jerusalem
the city that kills the prophets!'
Not a sound to sleep by under your own vine, this transient death.
Only a day ago and this was our nature reserve, sanctuary where
ducks may sit and squirrels may safely squirrel. But then the calendar.

The killers' tub is a khaki-mitted fist, a spandex balaclava
pulled over a boat and a pilot. He navigates the sunrise.   *Selah*

Maybe it's over now, for now, the trysting zone
between dark and light when the light
was in darkness and the darkness overcame it not :
it's stirred its stumps and gone.
Too bright now for killers.   *Selah*

Spirit, Spirit everywhere, nor any blank to blink.
Full, the tidal truth : full, full to the lips the cup, brim
brimmed and brimming, lapping at the rocks, it sock-socks in rocks
the sound of old dark boathouses, dark wood docks, last century's shores.

    Who has seen the Wind?
    Neither lens nor eye,
    But when the *fleuve* lets loose its waves
    The Spirit's passing by.

Spirit and Truth have wiped the shore of killers, but dinner was good
last night, perch, and *canard à l'orange* is one of our delights.
'The tongue is a small member, yet it boasts of great exploits....
The tongue is placed among our members as a world of iniquity.'

Calories are light pupating. The bowels are killers, they suck and
suck, tongues are their decoys attracting turnips, carrots, apples, beets,
peppers, pheasants, garlic, quince, *mâches*, chicken, chard, raisins,
pork chops, *pétoncles*, shallots, zucchini, Romaine, Windsor broad beans,
petits pois, petits fruits, baby spinach, lambs' tongues, what have I left out,
artichokes — O Jerusalem, Gethsemane, the garden that kills prophets!
All flesh is flesh.

Squash. Why is a good name an enemy action?
A harmless vegetable a gesture that kills with a shrug.
The grass reaper cometh. I hope Obama is praying.
The Spirit's passing through the ashes.
I meant the ash trees.

Not in Jerusalem; anywhere a witness, in Truth.
The Spirit and the water. *And* the blood.   *Selah*

TWO-FOLD THIS

Two ducks. Two chairs on the shore. Two trees either side.
    Two suns : one in the new-born sky, one on the water.
    Two persons in bed
        one bed, one house, one shore accordingly.
    Two rivers : one *fleuve*, one *ruisseau*, beside and before

      each heart and body
      each day to Thyself
      each night accordingly

one step at a time
one hour accordingly
one and then two
   out into time

both hearts and both bodies
both *fleuve* and *ruisseau*
both suns and both ducks
   all dwellers of shorelines.

      Be near me, uphold me,
      my treasure, my triumph

one step at a time
one minute according
   one hour in due course
      one sun a bit higher, sun's wealth's other sun
      on the ancient of waters in spillage of
  silver so spendthrift, so little like thrift
yet so much less like spending :
   bush burning
    self offering.

Still to this day
    by night accordingly
dreams of the hunting by killer no motive
    apparent the running
       full fathom....

Yet on this day
      one step in time
         from out this skete, out into this teeming

desert of graces
      with less than assurance but more than an absence of :
    cure of souls by confronting the forces.
         On tiptoe forth to essay the armed forces....

'Strength of contemplative
      [hare/saint] resistance'. So some have
         said who've turned hunters of 'word with
      enough of God in it' sheltering —
homing a hare
      is it like? granting a place to
         stand, Pennánt
      enshrining.

If by grace this wasteland
      serves
to dissolve the one curst and resolve the one blest
      to one left to where now two wholes make one flesh
        one bed, one house
           one shore
              one here
                one near
             this rise
           this day —
         if this,
      then
    this....

SEQUENCE FOR A FALL

i)   The river

What are you looking at?
The river.
What do you see?
Oh, nothing; the heron sitting on his rock
the surface of the river as slick as a ballroom
the sun making it to the top of a bunker of cloud : sunrise.

What are you watching?
The old heron on his old rock.
The young heron flew past near shore
   his slow wings scalloping the ribbon of river-air.
He points his toes like a dancer.

The old heron turns his back on the sunrise.
The tide has made it to his feet now
to his tail, to his body.
   Virginia Woolf.
I've never seen a heron float.

Black squirrel appropriates the littoral
poses on a pink rock, brief cameo, descends.
Early sun sets up into another cloud, a setup.

What are you seeing?
The river.
Old heron positions himself for lift-off
iconic profile towards shore, lifts off
skims the scalloped ribbon of river-air, off west.

How do you know he's old?
There are signs of 'old', we recognize them : unwillingness
   to shift, to budge, to say it's over
tide's in, that's it for the rock.

Tide takes over the set : a glistened stage.
Slicker than slick in the sunless sun.
Even the wind conspires for effect.
My rock disappears.

You have a rock?
Oh, I have a rock; the gulls
have squatters' rights but they didn't till a year ago — it
wasn't there. It took a crane.

It's my soap-box, from there I shout at the sun,
I preach my revivalist preachments to the crowded shore;
it's thick and more or less flat, box-like, my rock : an icon.

I don't actually shout.
I'm never on my rock, it's there in case.
There it is, nose disappearing under the flood, last air-hole.
Icon. My icon. That, from which lift-off.
That, to which anchors the 'leash of longing'.

What are you looking at now?
Nothing. The river.
What do you see?

Silence, deep breaths of it
    like wing-beats
        ribbon of breath flattened out
            like a single note, a sustained A^b
                a stave with nothing written on it
                    Menuhin's last breve, bow above the string
                    mirror of nothing, complete Cloud, what
                do I see? It's all there, all
            desire, the satisfaction that is and is not, Nyssa,
leash's anchor gone under, the Compleat Longing.

                                                        Selah

What are you looking at now?
The River.
What do you see?
Nothing. I will tell you a mystery :
God looks like a river.

Sequence for a Fall

ii)   I beheld her

I beheld her
as through a veil of ash
loosen her locks of hold on the world
let stream her ribboned ephemeral heyday
untether her inclement
weather make ready her departure;

let go her petals, her heartstrings, her held breath
disinvest her biding in this blue green globe in
its dark firmament
unabide as the breath abates
and the crests fall and the roll and pitch plane
and the tsunamis level and rake.

And I beheld all this
in the veil of ash as the wind dropped
and the whitecaps dissolved in the grey sea
and a voice began to wail
it came from Samoa it came from Somalia
it came from Syria, Sumatra, from Sudan
from St Pancras station
from all flesh whole
from out this own Pandora's chest
miniscule at first, almost inaudible
             while four leaves fell.

And the sun found it harder and harder
to get up in the morning
what was the point, he said, as he
skyrocketed off towers and Boeings and oil rigs and
deserts and skin day after day, just hit the snooze button
give me a bit longer, it's over the equinox
I've got it coming to me

so she lit her own skirts and swept through the tinderbox
and valleys flamed and houses vanished
people were disappeared in the booming conflagration
banknotes blazed to cinders
stopgaps and failsafes and safety nets fried in her flames
her hair caught fire and
I beheld her as through a veil of tears
        while four leaves fell.

And she had said I am leaving you my memory
and even that will burn to a crisp
and be buried in sand
what I have been will be no more
and it is not I who have done this thing
and it is not the Lord of the Universe who has done this thing.

Let me sing, do you know my swan? join in if you can, you
who loved me once, she said
as I watched her through the ashes' yellow veil
and there was a moan, it was not human, it came from towards the rocks
there was a nittering chittering as a bat died
and a pulsing pulse as something else became all ghost.
And she paused on the threshold with her song
        as four leaves fell.

And then she stepped off

it was dark there was no
human eye to see what had become of her
dark-years away but rumour has it
among the insects and the bdelloid rotifers and the microbes that
she is beautiful still somewhere, somewhere other
than here which is no more

that green blue globe, Lovelock'd cameo
a mere small tragic turn in the ultimately benign scenario.

And I was witness to this
down in the vale of ashes
        where four leaves fall.

SEQUENCE FOR A FALL

iii) The dumbshow prologue

Anish Kapoor and Robert Lepage have this in common with
latitude 46°42' at longitude 71°85' from 6:13 AM to 6:32 AM
30 days past the fall equinox with 10 days to go till
Eastern Standard Time *anno Domini* 2009 :
the installation art of the ephemeral.

At 7:13 the crow caws twice to announce 7:14 and the sun's one headlight
peaks the horizon, starts barrelling up its tracks, one-eyed sun-train.
Takes him 4 minutes to roll into full view full round, Ash Tree Imogen
        fleetingly his tangent then off he goes, paler and paler
chugging off into the sunrise with today's post.
Anish Kapoor's wax.

But that's not it.
It's one hour before, for 19 minutes from 6:13 *ante meridiem* —
the dumbshow prologue : the red of all fall leaves bleeding
        into the skyline like a cicatrice of joy
love's bright bruise, love's bruised flesh, sky as flesh
        with only light, with barely
light in the blanketing dark, the child pulling the eiderdown over its head
to see the firefly fire up, that joy of first light in dark's *coulisses*
        black velvet's secrets
or the man who mapped much of north-west Canada pouring
        his fortune and his life into that particular cartography of truth that
        nobody would buy and
        throwing it into the last fire that kept him warm before
        all his resources ran out.
Precious ephemeral fire.

Not the chug-chug-chug of the train, but the red promise, the waiting
        on the platform.
Or the memory of it.

Kapoor would say the memory is the art.
Bishop Berkeley would say it's all in His head.
The broken bread says
      it was so
      once and again
      it was so
      only ever once and
      again and again
for about 19 minutes, maybe 9, the canon sounds
and then it's over, love's bruise heals
as if it never was.

But it was.
Love's anamnesis.
Why should everything last, indeed? Mantelpieces don't last,
pictures over mantelpieces don't stop time its dissolution,
      the bread breaks, the light
      breaks, that's it that's all.
      Given for you.
      'Remember meeeeeeeeeeee….'.…
Cut.

SEQUENCE FOR A FALL

iv) Wasn't this about fire?

What a rum thing worship is. Little knots of people
aping the real thing 'as it is in heaven', a cocktail of inter-
congratulatory self-satisfaction. Pour over ice, forget to shake.

Forgive us, Lord. I hope we'll recognize it when we get there,
our palettes not too jaded with cheap liturgy, mistaken
intentions. Wasn't this about fire, about blood, about Word?

What we get is *storgē*. Churched, we take your Body in vain.
I know, I know, one must begin somewhere. I know, I know,
behind the comfortable pew the private desolation.

And your blessèd monk said 'a privy stirring of love', as if
its hiddenness were its validity. But Lord, but Lord!
Your waves do better, your birds. Consider the ravens.

Or okay stick to the waves. As your sun illuminates
this manuscript of holy writ in grain and gleam, the waves
                                        all robed in white
                            navy capped with chipped ice
                    rushing as lit fire, as coal catching spark
            head pell-mell downstream as if liturgy is nothing if not
        moving, if not blood-racing, bough-bending, *flèche*-shooting
speed. It's high! But this?

I know I know, low too, and this
is low, I know I know, humble. But it's
what's *more* than humble, *more* than prostrate

it's what goes to the stake, what feeds
the movement of the flames, we know whose flames, we know
Polycarp's, Ignatius his lions. God! Would they have recognized us?

We play at this. If stones could speak.
If ravens could participate. If waves could teach.
'Where was this unscripted choreography learned?'

Give us this day our 'choreography of promise'
teach us to pray
to dance, to wave, to flame : 'Why not become fire?'

Fingertips would do, would feel the vibration
of the butterfly in Tokyo, buzz with the 'om' of indicative prayer
song would do, from the entrails up the throat out the breath

anything, anything but this game of mistaken identity
pastiche of false echoes of false consciousness
'sans eyes, sans taste, sans everything'. A clue! A clue!

For *this* the sun rises? For *this* the glory passes by the cleft rock?
I had rather break stale bread on that
wet flat rock table in the sand in the *fleuve* in your name as your priest

than fake the gift of heaven in a smug cult.
I had rather be a doorkeeper.... One day in thy courts
is better than a thousand....

Can indignation be forgiven? heaven
forfend this scrupulous distaste?
Bear with me, Lord, bear me, I can hardly bear myself.

'Be near me, uphold me, my treasure, my triumph.'
'Yet a little while.'
'Let me never be confounded.'

SEQUENCE FOR A FALL

v) One sunrise he reached

One sunrise he reached for a bottle of wine
to assuage the grief of a life flickering out whose feeble
incandescence had gypped the light of its truth.
Or so he thought.

Sunrise mocks us. '*We're* still at it', each sun says, 'while *you*...!'
As many moons catch in the branches of many trees, so
many suns catch in the throat : sobs that gag on the rule that
light recapitulates light.

Oh? says the alcohol. What's this then?
This thing that doesn't happen new every morning
this guttering, guttural-sputtering bulb dying to a hiss
of its own making?

I am sorry for me. Aren't we all?
Who's got the agility any longer to dodge this list of unaccomplishments
this clinging to the light switch for one last evening's read, learn, one last
evening's Inwardly Digest Truth's light?

It's called an *interrupteur* in French and oh, it is that, it is that.
We were just getting going. Just warming up,
our light converting to heated discussion, print, sauce,
something to show for all the hours.

Our power went last night.
Hydro Québec had to send a truck.
A brief reminder *ex machina* of where we are without that juice.
Nothing, no water, no heat, no cooking, no seeing. Sans everything.

The dark night of the cloud.
The wine lied. In *vino* was not *veritas* that spoke. Read, learn :
'No man by his own works, seem they never so good...',
never so published, never so read, or clapped.

So hard an ascesis. 'I am a worm and no man'?
No, that's not it. When we fall from sucking on our virtues
like leeches from salt, we fall not from but *into* a
space that doesn't, we think, suit.

The coat's too generous, we
sulk, we trip on the hem, *his* hem.
But the me I'm sorry for's not me,
it's my alter-icon, my idol. Little children,

keep yourself from idols.
The power went back on and the sun
rose, yes. But the *interrupteur* shines
in the dark : remember, O man.

'It's not I', says faith. 'He went that-a-way'.
Nothing doing, we say, and mean 'I won't',
mean give us this day our daily word count,
our daily thought, our day's works.

But faith says he went that-a-way. And we writhe
in our power-outage as if zapped by an electric chair.
We are the no-name brand. Get over it.
In that last resort, there will be no mirrors.

ALL SAINTS' EVE

Sanctus,   Sanctae,   Sancti
shanti   shanti   shanti
Holy   Holy   Holy

  the full moon
rising on All Saints' Eve like a sun.
'Om' says the moon.

haloes aureoles nebulae

  round the head
 round the trunk
round the *corps,* sheaths of endurance, helmets of holiness
the bubble people in their loricas of luminescence
  in their saintmobiles
 in a world of pain, on the cutting edge of sanctity
  they ride in
 lancing the heart, the wound.
O quanta qualia! O great heart! Break —
Christ slivered into a million saints.

We get it wrong. All our dear hymns. The saints don't wait.

It's *now*. Into their incontaminate bubbles they go
 parcelling up heaven and perambulating with it
heaven on rollerblades
  come to a street near you.

Abelard not so far wrong — *O quanta qualia*
'how immense, how wonderful' the unfinished unfinishing
Sabbaoth, the *éternuement éternel* that passeth all imagining you can,
    Ceci n'est pas un sunrise?
  kidding!
 utterly giddy with begotten glee
begoddening
  as beseems.

But it's not then, though also then.
We get this wrong.
It's in the now of the allthewayness of the H word
   that the H word figures
not in the exit from the great tribulation (though it was great)
        or from the trouble-and-strife (saintly rhyming slang for 'life')

it's the resurrection of the body *now* into
   ambulatory temples padding about corridors or
          blading down the Champs Élysées or
      rough-sleeping it with the Radiance
post-hole augering in Rwanda for well springs of living.

Job the Sequel.
Googols of chattels a stammering substitute for
grief   (of the suffering of the waste of the lost)   made
   holy here, 'rectified'
      with dark peace made, dark peace made.
Wholed   joyed   Jobed.
   Job's Sequence. *Else.*
Here be somewhere's *Else.*

Om.
Holy   Holy   Holy
               are the saints in light
in their infinitely large haloic bubble
      wherein
'semper celebrat superna curia' — by which for sure Abelard
      did not mean the paraphernalia of Vaticania
but where desire meets its match
   where desire is endlessly on the up and up
      yet endlessly met
   in endless celebrations of sempeternal Last Suppers
never begun at the soup and never arriving at the nuts
      100-proof spirits
   silly with repetition like some
tongue-twister mastered endlessly kidstuff endlessly kidding.

Those who have most urgently yearned
those who have cried *'Love!'*   *'God!'*   *'Help!'*
long enough and inaudibly enough and over and over

God! Love! Help!   *God! Help! Love!*   *Love! Help! God!*
      heart on sleeve
        till they
Help God Love   and this
           in despite of
        not because of
        or if because of also in spite of
    heroics darkening pain grief terror cruelty red
     martyrdom :

those are they, all robed in
the daily disposition of the mantic heart, the over and over of
        having done with all that other
         stuff, that decoy 'life'
and being daily disposed to the quotidian up-and-up
    for better for worse
       for richer for poorer
          for here and now :
             meeked and married
and cut the losses

those are they, doing the Breakthrough
        line dancing.
It's the best company in the world *in the world*, the communion of saints
         light and delight breaking, *à jamais* breaking
   in endlessly sustained sacrament.

Getting our heads round sainthood.
Hoods up, haloes on! — your sainthood round your head, hup!

Och! no, I know, luv, I know. And not by act
the H word. And not by deed, the portion.
H is for happen, for
dawn.

Omm
   mmoon-glory.
      Sancti sancti sancti
O quanta qualia. O Heart, rise.

PADDLE-TO-THE-SEA

He was hauling in halyards of peace over his right shoulder
peace by the fistful, the whole nine yards.
    I saw it. I was there. There is such a thing as witness.
I was witness to the Great Transition in the kitchen chair.

'O Son of God, do a miracle for me, and change my heart,' he
had prayed and the Lord had. In 15th century Ireland.
    Thanks to that one, again now.
Six centuries more of clouds of witness.

O Lord, open Thou our hearts
and our mouths shall slurp in Thy peace.
    I tipped the scales, the glass. I was the tipping point.
The Holy Three use agency as they can.

Miracles may, and may not, be interventions.
They may, and may not, be the outpouring of the
    Holy Impotence from the Cross, the
Son reigning from the Tree,

bubbles that bubble up from the bottom of the pan
you may or may not have put on to boil, of the flute
    you may or may not have poured. Part of the same.
'I am thirsty' from the Tree.

Lanyards or nails, we are bound to this outpouring of extinction
and grief *sancti sancti sancti* as if, lashed hand and foot
    to a log and floating down-*fleuve*, at any time we might be
rolled over by the tide and there, face in the *fleuve*, we'd be : not.

The Holy Impotence is Love all the way, the unfathomable, the *fleuve*.
This is what He came for, the Sun, in this great expanse
    of species and sentience, that we might float, the Lady of Shallot,
to our watery graves as our 'deliverance shines out like the dawn'.

Day is the ultimate liturgy. It's peace that's invisible in the dark
like our feet. Step by triune step, webbed foot by webbed
off we go
    Paddle-to-the-Sea, stroke by stride by wade by flap
        half-blind into the ultimate liturgy :
            acolytes of the Holy Impotence.

VERS TOI : ADVENT

The banks of brume are back :
ducks
    geese
        Abram setting out for he knows not what
        he knows not where —
'Va pour toi', vers toi-même, the elusive self beyond self's distance lens.
Bull's-eyed heifer sun sacrificed to
a fog of unknowing.

Foghorn and frost, the hunt — where will they tell me to stop?
What will I find?
Will I still know you?
Will I still love you?
'When I'm sixty-four…'.
Vers toi — my sky! my sky!

The more the sun the less to see.
        Slits of ice
    all hard light in the liquid flow of day
creep downstream
apologies for cold. Frost's fire and ice.

Pen-line of light along the far shore a
fluke of cloud-break, piping on the
    chasuble of the fleuve —
        advent-coloured
the bonnie banks of brume.

'The reredos was not/ an ecclesiastical adornment/ of symbols'
went the poem, 'but plain glass' — which has shaped à jamais
the way our bodies wear this vestment of 'house'
    our way of holding
        to this place.

« *C'est au déclin du soleil; une torpeur est tombée sur Abram* »
      and his
smoke-pot and burning torch perform the sacrificial
      animal ritual
        under the Watchers and the Holy Ones
            Abram in the 'deep and terrifying darkness'
      going through the motions.

What I shall show you.
        As the grains of sand.
            As the stars in the sky.

Going through God's motions.
God going through Abraham's.
'When I'm sixty-four.'
It's all un-...
        Ophelia undoing Shallot's web of weave
        and these bonnie bonnie
            banks of brume a day's rest between night terrors.

RAMEAU DARK

Ô Nuit! This is a Rameau dark. *'Viens apporter*
à la terre/ le calme enchantement/
de ton mystère' : darkness affective,
darkness as you like it, darkness to taste, vintage dark —
    the love of shadows caressing.

Is shadow's dream sweeter than hope? The Little Prince
    who comes would not say so, if he could speak.
'What is truth?' 'What is hope?' is as easy
as shrugging, a very pretty melancholy.
    Or worse : Plato's cave.

Ô Nuit! There is no sound tonight
    but the choral replay in my head. Truly there is
no sound, my ears ring with the silence
deep as the channel of the *fleuve*
    for seagoing.

All is calm, all is, in fact, star-lit, is, in fact, bright
with the late moon — late in all late's ways
    as Copenhagen meets to attempt to resist
the damage we are capable of. 'What' after all
    'is truth?'

O Night! *'O! laisse encore à la terre'* a bit of its future imperfect
    the outplaying of its incarnation
the calm acknowledgment of its mystery. Enchantment
is a byproduct, not the thing itself. Beware bewitchedness.
    Beware the shrug.

Ô Nuit! — but your beauty, your fair beauty! Seeing
with not seeing. And he comes, they
    say, the astonishing visitor, the man who came to dinner
and *was* dinner, as a mother is for her breastfed.
    Pelican icon.

In the night. It is in the night that he comes
   into the night. In such a night as this
the fair Jessica
with her Lorenzo on the starlit bank, the bonnie
   banks of dark

did love each other truly and in hope
and in hope of a third one
   their own coming into the world
     coming to his own
in such a night as this, all mystery
   foretelling.

'O! laisse encore à la terre' the voices
   whose concerted music signifies and perhaps emits
'l'espérance' : the angels coming, the night, Copenhagen
dispelling, and the choral replay
    with the children
   singing in the front row new to performance
    holding their own.

DECEMBER'S FAITHFUL ECLIPSE

December's faithful eclipse of the sun.
The animals know, sleep it off
      in our ceilings under the rooves.
From our woods come *petits bois* for the fire, squirrels for the eaves.
Our heat heats the neighbourhood.

The prolonged Holy Saturday of Advent :
hibernating in hell and despairing not.
      The dreams of squirrels.
Not at all preferring a dream of shadows (sweet succubus melancholy) to
a flint fact of hope. The math is night over dream equals glint.

O Nuit blows in from the east, the first tempest.
This is better than Stratford; *pace* Chris Plummer, we *have* our tickets :
      the window is a proscenium is a storm
      howling.
      Job doing Lear doing Tempest.
The royal eclipse of the sun.

A window onto an absence. The Coming echoes
with absence like a house after the movers, like a school hall with
      no children, how things were
      when this looked big, you so small. But now.
Only the echo is large.

Why is the Incarnation so much like the Resurrection?
The squirrels know, not I. Solstice
      pivots on a wisdom : 'the emotion/ that almost
startles us/ when a happy thing *falls.*'
And can it be, and can it be

that he had *happy* hours in hell? knowing
the wrists of Adam, Eve, knowing
      the tug of roots, his arms dragging them to light
with a glint fact of hope, with lanyards
of divine baler-twine, his brace of dead : show-handling.

December : Adam and Eve's month. The long wait.
'Keep your mind in hell and despair not.' There :
      perfect pitch   blackout
as the proscenium master-switch is thrown.
Nothing but the wind over the waters

      before the brooding
looking for where to tabernacle, where to lay the egg of civilization
      the race that must be won.
As transient as a nest in straw is the world, an eave
      to be won over to light : December knows, not I.

All's Eve.
And the brave holiday lights on the shivering trees
      mark the absence.

MESSE DE MINUIT

Driving home from the *messe de minuit*
    fog off the *fleuve*
        a flagon of it resting in the palm of the land
           then we come clear.

There's our house
    our berth on earth we briefly
        belong to
           while driving home

the long way
    through the minutiae
        remembering the Great Blue
           the Ideal Heron passing downstream

deliberate line scissoring the mist
    faultless and slow
        airline between Earth and non-Earth
        airbrushed, Nyssa-wing

one more feather's one more hair numbered, accounted :
    the 'for' of it.
        We home here for a while
          the *Anse*

frozen over   *repassé* flat
    hard   cold   the Ideal Iron   *Anse*
      andiron for the log
        in the eye, the end-on sun logging on

remember how the sun?
    a burning mote
        rolled up the cortex of the window?
          That was some day.

A window is an eye is an icon.
   Promise I won't blink.
      'O Earth return!' one holy writ.
        The pieces are falling out.

The heron-rock also
   hard   cold   poised mid-   flight and frozen
     stitched into the shutter speed
       as the tide flees. O tide return.

Remember how the sun
   innocent of power
     cauterized the horizon
       scalded the peeled eye

'Here, send me,' the lips sear earth's air
   'Let me go there,' he had uttered
     and the evening
       and the morning were the first millennium.

Trapped in our atmosphere
   love won't let him leave
     here, he says, let me
       over and over, while

over and over shouldering
   the weight of it
     earth
       crowded with death

biology spinning off its axis
   the wobble of the precession
     of the particulars, he laying down
       his life over and over

once for all innocent
   of power, the Holy One
     laying it all down the evening
       and all down the morning being the second

millennium, remember how
    the sun?
        Oh, yes! And how
           always at dawn, before the rise

a bird or three ply a way
    across the *fleuve* at right angles
        to the rise?
           Clear, before the blinding.

Oh, yes! I remember
    I loved it.
        That was just before the birth
           right?

I believe so.
    Driving home from midnight
        desire's wing
           and 'kids do the darnedest

things…!' Look! How'd that kid
    get in the *barn* in the *feed* trough?
        'Kids will be kids'
           driving home the point that

'what I do is me, for this I came'.
    Here, eat me eat me : the Holy Imperative
        of Wonderland. You are
           what you eat. Son within.

(And all of this is done
    with his hands tied to a crossbar
        little Hercules in his cradle
           'They shall not hurt or destroy in all my holy mountain'.)

It comes clear in a barncat's cradle :
    What I do not do
        is me, the Baby, for this infant impotence I came :
           I Am the Holy Un-One.

Kids do the darnedest things.

One last crèche

I knew it! I've caught them at it again
       the living room furniture on all fours
              chairs, divan, chesterfield, even the dining room table
      and its diaconal attendants
all holding their tableau round the mystery

participatory spectators
       at the hearth of the living fire.
              They are ox and ass — I knew it! How still, these *meubles*
       waiting between cuds with no impatience to be chewing
this could last forever

the birth having been,
       the surprised shepherds having come
              and gotten used to the idea by now, and the gracious cold
       freezing on with the fire at the heart and
we are waiting for the Wise Men.

Wisdom is in the air
       been hanging around for well over a week now.
              They will come, we're not holding our breath, we know
       they will come. We are holding our breath
only because we are not impatient

so little impatient even to chew that
       we can see no improvement on this shining hour
              not one more breath to draw to fill this to full.
       This is the Atonement for all animals.
We are satisfied.

Put the injustice (just for now) on hold
       the master's whip, the lost calf, the scapegoat, the barbed wire
              the drought and how we camels were turned away from the
       wells to die in the desert, were shot when we wouldn't
stay away — the wells insufficient for satisfaction.

All the deaths, the pelican insurance chick, the lion cubs the new king
        kills to reign, the dodos, the dinosaurs, the pogroms, the drownings
                the famines, the earthquakes, the evil, the hate, the thorn
        in the paw infected, how can he ever make satisfaction for
such a creation, for so much suffering, such wrath

as we creatures feel towards our Maker?
        If he could speak. But he can only
                take on growing, till the baby is a grown man
        and puts his arms on the crossbar, hands up! the Holy Impotence
to be shot at daybreak by the firing squad.

We played our part.
        Oh so many wraths ago.
                And yet here we are, bewondered :
        knowing 'young' when we see it, the young of others,
letting the sheep's lamb

nurse at the heifer's teat, letting
        the kitten pull the goat's ear, letting
                the child roll in the straw and stepping carefully round
        or nuzzling it, for curiosity, for pleasure : here, again.
Here be Young. Here be How it all Begins

With Us
        Here
                When Yet a Little While is All
        in All and
We have been Satisfied.

That's what the *meubles* sang that night silent —
        unmoving movable creature-crèche of four-leggèd
                sofas, armchairs — seats and backs and arms and end-games
        holding their own round the *foyer* now ardent coals
of glowing : of their own, burnt there.

All flesh is wood
  is ash is fire's seed of spark
    of dawn scattered and abounding
  on good earth and bad.
Is that so!

Whether it's so
  I cannot tell, the movables know.
    That's what they said.
  They've made it up
with their Maker.

Job too.
Job done.